# The Happiness Triangle

*Dieudonne D'amour Nordkvist*

Dieudamour AB
Galoppstigen 18E
SE 653 48 Karlstad
Tel: +46 (0)76 200 40 70
www.dieudamour.com



Cover design by Stamatis latridis (wearetejp.se)
Inlay and illustrations by Tom Karlsson
Printed by Universitetstryckeriet, Karlstad
ISBN : 978-91-639-8129-6

# Table of contents


**Foreword** 8

Why is this book necessary?

Involvement

What are the benefits?

**Preface** 10

**Introduction** 11

**Chapter 1: Is it possible?** 13

Winners and losers

What's wrong with society's "happiness" model?

**Chapter 2: What is happiness?** 16

Is pleasure happiness?

If happiness is not pleasure, then what is happiness?

What are your basic happiness needs?

**Chapter 3: Maslow's pyramid** 19

Maslow

Aristotle's viewpoint

A new model

**Chapter 4: Aligning human needs with our goals** 24

What is the meaning of these specific angles?

**Chapter 5: What are health and wealth?** 27

Thoughts about health

Thoughts about wealth

**Chapter 6: What is worth?** 35

Thoughts about worth

1. Purpose

2. Relationships

3. Contribution

**Chapter 7: The 180-degree rule of sustainable happiness model**  41

Relationship between worth and wealth

The relationship between worth and health

Relationship between health and wealth

**Chapter 8: Being busy and being happy**  46

**Chapter 9: The three rules of the Happiness Triangle**  50

What is the challenge?

Models of Happiness Triangles

What about you?

Calculating your angles

My Happiness Triangle drawing

**Chapter 10: Three guidelines for an equilateral Happiness Triangle**  57

Guideline 1: Have both commitment and belief

Guideline 2: Be positive and curious

Guideline 3: Take responsibility

Change or complain?

**Chapter 11: Individual growth**  64

The road to maturity

**Chapter 12: Conclusion**  68

**Quotes**  72

**Your assistance is appreciated**  74

**Acknowledgments**  75

**About the author**  76

# Foreword

**Why is this book necessary?**

I wish I could guarantee right here, right now, that everyone will achieve their full measure of happiness, worth, and potential before the time of departure to the great beyond. But I cannot do that, for I would be committing a very large injustice. Many people die leaving behind untapped wealth. Some of those reading this book will not fulfill their purpose in life because they choose not to put some of the ideas and tips that I describe here into practice. But before I go further, I wish to advise all those seeking quick riches through gambling, theft, ritual killings, bank robbery, and all other forms of ill-gotten wealth to stop reading this book, because it will not help you. This book is for those who believe in something deep within; those who have a burning desire to succeed in achieving their highest happiness and success but who need some guidance in the process.

This book is for those who are stuck in a 9-to-5 job and want a change for a better life, or for those whose dreams keep knocking once they close their eyes and fall sleep at night, only for them to vanish once they wake up early in the morning. This book is for you. You'll learn why you are still at a point that you have been trying to move past, and what the exit route from such a vicious circle is.

**Involvement**

To be happy, you must be doing something. You must be involved in something you love in order to fulfill your goals in life. We all have to do this, knowing that it's a challenge. Still, we must persist in solving problems, expressing our creativity, getting into the state of "flow," and feeling like we are taking action. So how do we get involved? This is covered in Chapter 6: What is Worth?

**What are the benefits?**

Within a short time after reading this book, you will begin to see important changes in your life that will create a better and clearer picture of what you need for health, and for a never-ceasing flow of happiness. You will find your happiness increasing, which means that your relationships, your career, your goals, and your beliefs may also change so that they can match the new You. Your life can be full of joy and satisfaction. If you aspire to experience amazing improvement and growth within yourself, this book will start you on that path. Follow its teachings thoughtfully, carefully absorb and practice its principles and formulas, and take your time in creating your current Happiness Triangle. Doing so will let you see where improvements are needed. You will view yourself becoming a person of greater usefulness who wields an expanded influence for a better future for your family and new generations to come.

# Preface

I am grateful to have witnessed two major life events. One was when my daughter was born, and the other was when my mother passed away. Those events left me in a complete state of shock that caused both pain and joy. I had never felt those emotions so strongly before. They taught me lessons that have changed my life—in how I prioritize my time and use the other resources that are in my control.

When my daughter was still in the womb, I had a serious question about life in general. Specifically, how can a baby breathe in the kind of environment that exists in the womb? I asked around, but no one knew the answer. So I started to research it on the internet. As it turns out, a fetus doesn't breathe the way we do in this world. That only begins when the baby is born. On the day of birth, as all first-time parents, I was in a panic and out of my mind. For the first time in my life, I felt useless, not knowing what to do or what to expect. It was so difficult for both her mother and me to just relax and let it be. When she was born, it all happened in a very short moment. It was like a miracle. She brought so many tears, and so much joy and happiness into my life. Everything I was doing, or the fears I was feeling, changed the moment she cried for the first time. What really happened in that moment was that the Universe gave life to our baby when she inhaled oxygen. One of the keys of our life is the air that we breathe. A year later, my mother passed away. Her death put a brutal end to all my fine projects. She succumbed to a long, painful illness from which there was no hope of recovery. We knew this from the beginning, and so I thought I was prepared, expecting her death, but it still came as a terrible blow. I went into a long depression. I loved her very much, but I had not spent much time with her.

On the day she died, I was in the same room with her. She was breathing, and breathing, and suddenly she took her last breath and then it was over. The air that had entered into her body when she was born left her, and she left this world. This is the air that we people, nature, and animals, share and breathe together. We take it for granted that we will have this air forever.

# Introduction

After experiencing the events I just described, I realized that while one event brought me joy, the other took away that same joy. It brought to the surface deeper feelings that lasted a long time. So I started to ask myself the important questions that everyone asks at some point: What is the meaning of this life that we are living? What is the goal of my life? What is the relationship between those two events?

I realized that my life has a start point and an end point, and it is incredibly interesting to get to know myself and who I am. I started questioning why we are given the chance to live on this Earth. **I discovered that the goal of our life is to feel happiness and take care of our bodies.** We are to keep this goal in mind until that day comes when we take our last breath on this Earth. When you are born, you bring joy and positive feelings—or energy—to the world and your family. This energy or feeling is what you can call "happiness."

When you die, you leave negative feelings and energies behind, which can be called "sadness." Those two feelings are a part of our life. They are inseparable; they walk side by side. If one leaves an area, the other will follow and take its place. I began to read books of philosophies from people like Gandhi, Maslow, Aristotle, and many more. Most of them agreed that if the meaning of life lies in a commongoal of human beings, then it is happiness that is the goal. My journey to discover the secret formula of happiness started on that day. I was in a depression from losing my mother, but at the same time, I have my daughter, who is a source of joy and happiness. I knew by then that I had grasped something special and different. I wanted to be happy and healthy, just like everyone else. But my body and feelings were not cooperating after the loss of my mother. I had to be hospitalized. I couldn't believe that at age 39, my health was in such bad shape! My relationships with my family and work were not good either. In getting out of my body and analyzing how I felt and what was causing it, I made a list of things that are my sources of happiness—those people, places, or things that will help me maintain happiness and/or change any negative feelings into positive ones. While creating this exercise of listing of my sources of happiness, I recognized that other people, perhaps because of circumstances beyond their control, may also be suffering. Their basic starting point might be as low as mine, or worse. Good health and sufficient income are not always available to everyone, through no fault of their own. But a certain percentage of people in this world live wonderful lives, raise happy, healthy children, and are alive until they are 80 or 90 years old. "Why can't I be one of them? Does anyone have to give me that permission?" I asked myself. Since then, my primary goal has been to increase the likelihood that I'll be one of those remarkable people who can achieve greatness and who makes a real difference in other people's lives. This goal is very much in my own hands—not in the hands of my doctor, my wife, or my children. It is my own responsibility. I realized that to achieve my full potential, I had to free myself, as much as possible, from randomness and uncertainty. I had to learn how to question and analyze my daily activities, my happiness and what it is, and the cause-and-effect relationships between what I wanted and how I was going to get it. **I had to take complete control over every part of my life and create my own path to happiness.**

# Chapter 1
**Is it possible?**

From an early age, I heard and was taught that if you earn a lot of money, you will be happy. You probably heard this when you were a child, or maybe you have told this to your own children. *"If you (insert accomplishment that results in a lot of money), you will have all it takes to be happy!"*

But is that true? Do your children have all it takes? I mean, do they understand what you mean by that? Of course not. True happiness can be achieved no matter what your starting conditions are. As we go along, we wish that we could control every element of our life, including the ability to be happy. The good news is that we can! This true happiness is a sustainable, long-term condition. It is not a short, fake, and temporary joy, such as looking at the world through rose-colored glasses—thinking that things are better than they actually are. The problem is that human beings do not have the slightest idea of what happiness truly is, let alone how to achieve it. Many people say that anyone can be happy. But then they add one more requirement: "If you work hard!"

**Winners and losers**

But it does not really matter if you work hard; at the end of the day, you will be classified into a societal category. These are not based on race or religion, and society groups people into only two contrasting classes: Winners and Losers. Over and over, society tells us the same thing: *If you work hard enough to become a winner, then you will be happy and recognized.* But the strange thing is, there is always only one winner. That means, therefore, that the rest of humankind must be losers. The odds are stacked against you: You will lose the game society is playing. Not because you are an idiot, but because the probability of you actually becoming a winner is so low. This, in turn, affects you, as well as the rest of your life and your future. Will you become a sellout? Imagine someone who has reached the age of 40 years old. They are not married and do not

have any kids—no nice job, no car, nor a house. Imagine a 65-year-old
person who also does not possess the items mentioned above. Most people
will immediately place those people in the "Loser's Box," where they can
feel sorry for them. Of course, they insist that those people cannot possibly
be happy and that they need to be taken care of. But when we achieve these
things, we tell ourselves that we feel happy because we have succeeded.
Right? Or are we blinded by this self-congratulatory mechanism? Do we
consistently put on our rose-colored glasses and tell ourselves: "I am
worthy because of what I have worked for. I am happy."

### What's wrong with society's "happiness" model?

The problem is that the single model humankind has created for happiness
is this: Get up early, study, exercise, and work hard. Like me, you may have
used this example as a model for success and the way to achieve happiness.
We'll talk more about success later, but the basic teaching most of us
absorbed is that those who do not follow the formula of "get up early,
study, exercise, and work hard" are useless or losers. Society requires us
to work hard like a stone, or other beast of burden. But a stone doesn't
have a life. **Every human has a potential to be happy and to live
a happy life.** The only issue is that no one knows how—beyond that
well-known formula—and you and I are already becoming aware that it
is not a clear path to achieving happiness. The reason that we are in this
world is to be happy. Nothing else. It requires much knowledge and exercise
to achieve this level of joy, but it is not impossible. Some say it is complicated.

Yes, it is. If it wasn't, life might be much simpler, but it would also be less
robust and enjoyable. This complexity means that in any attempt to achieve
happiness, the formula will need to be adjusted to fit the individual and
their circumstances. One person may have health but is lacking self-worth.
Another person may be sublimely confident but is lacking financially.
The formula is sound, but two different people will create two different
personal Happiness Triangles. However, they will use the same concept
to create them. This is the reason that I wrote this book—so you can absorb
the book's knowledge and, for the first time, access a single formula that

is conceptually simple and will work to increase happiness for you,
your family, and everyone else around. As I mentioned in the introduction,
not everyone has the conditions in place to achieve happiness. For some
people, circumstances beyond their control may conspire to make
it impossible. Good health and sufficient income are not always available
through no fault of their own. For this method to work as intended,
it is necessary that the reader already have a financial support system
in place and also be in basically good health, with no underlying medical
conditions. Can we improve our definition of happiness further from simply
saying it is not like looking at life through rose-colored glasses?

# Chapter 2
**What is happiness?**

Possibly the best place to start defining happiness is by explaining what it is not. Many people believe that happiness is having fun at a party, feeling the excitement of new experiences, feeling the thrill and passion of sex, or tasting the delights of a fine meal. If we wish for something and then receive it, that gives us joy. These are all wonderful experiences to be cherished and cultivated, but they do not define the happiness discussed in this book. Actually, these experiences define pleasure. They are occurrences to have and let pass, like a meal to savor and then digest, or a party to enjoy and then let it wind down. It is the passion to enjoy, and the warm afterglow to linger in.

**Is pleasure happiness?**
If there is one word that most of us think of when we consider happiness, it is "pleasure." This emotion is fleeting, and it must be so if it is to continue to please us. If we have specific joyful experiences all the time, then our brain will adapt and turn that pleasure into a routine. Once that happens, it takes even more time to make us feel good again. **Chasing pleasure is not happiness.** Pleasure is, however, one of our essential human needs. Love, tasty food and drink, humor and laughter, joyful experiences, the feeling of gratitude—and let's not forget sex—are all experiences of pleasure. It is a "happiness" that is based upon satisfying the basic needs within our control. A word of caution here: pleasurable experiences release addictive chemicals in the brain. Too much of a good thing can create an unhealthy addiction that interferes with other aspects of our happiness in many ways. Remember, the key to happiness is by meeting all our needs and goals, not just the pursuit of pleasure. But real happiness is something very different from pleasure. It is a feeling that is closer to satisfaction and fulfillment. One marker that clearly distinguishes pleasure from

happiness is that pleasure is a temporary feeling, whereas happiness
is a state that can be maintained for a long time.

**If happiness is not pleasure, then what is happiness?**
In this book, happiness is defined as: **A long-term state of mind that is
achieved when we are in control of our life, or when we know where
we are and where we are going.** When we have the power and freedom
to choose, to affect what we want to do, to make important decisions for
ourselves, and take responsibility to independently affect our own feelings
and emotions, then we can achieve happiness. In other words… Happiness
comes during the journey we choose to take to satisfy and fulfill our
life goals. Happiness equals a feeling of contentment: that life is exactly
just as it should be. Perfect happiness, even enlightenment, comes when
we are in control and have freedom, knowing that we are on the way to fulfill
and achieve all of our needs and goals. Happiness is like love. It expands
to fill the space we make available for it.

**What are your basic happiness needs?**
Individual needs vary based on genetics, in how we were raised, and the
variety of our life experiences. That complex combination is what makes
each of us unique, both in our individual needs and every other aspect of
what makes us the person we are. We may each be complex beings,
but as humans, that identification provides the foundation on which we can
discover our essential human needs. Just as we are all born looking human
on the outside, we share common basic goals on the inside. Where we differ
is how strongly we feel about each of those goals and needs.

What are my needs? What are the goals of my life?
If we want to be happy, all we have to do is make sure that we are in line
with society's formula for happiness, that we have control, and that our needs
and goals are fulfilled. Right? That sounds simple enough, but the question
then becomes, "What are those needs?" That's where things start to get a bit
more complex. You see, for thousands of years, philosophers, psychologists,

and scientists have tried to find an answer to this essential question about our basic needs. And because humans like simple answers, many have tried to answer these questions in simple ways. The answer provided is always that we must fulfill one major need, sometimes two. Eventually, some suggested there are five essential needs. The pressure was on to keep the number of essential needs aslow as possible, to keep the formula simple and memorable. This theory leads to some interesting questions:

–What if that effort to simplify the issue causes us to miss the point?
–What if, in the desire to find this one essential need, the actual needs of real, complex humans, like you and me, are being overlooked–just because people want to have a simple, bite-sized answer?
–What if the answer isn't in fulfilling this need, that need, or even those five needs, but rather, something completely different than the equation set forth above?
–What if Plato, Aristotle, the Hedonists, and Maslow were basically all wrong regarding their definitions of happiness?
–What if we could integrate thousands of years of philosophical inquiry with current modern psychology and neuroscience?
–What if we examined the needs that are fulfilled by the major world religions?

The final question is: What would our basic goals and needs look like if we used all of the sources listed above? There may be overlaps between scientific and psychological solutions. Would the answer be simple enough to understand? Yes! This effort has been realized in a rational, logical manner that's easy to examine. Do you want to know what it is?

# Chapter 3
**Maslow's pyramid**

To be able to understand this new model of happiness, let's look into the wisdom of the Eastern and Western world. Both consider happiness to be an important goal of life. Maslow called the five essentials "human needs" and presented them in a pyramid, and Aristotle had some interesting things to say regarding happiness. You will be able to see how these models are useful and how they also need to be improved.

**Maslow**

Abraham Harold Maslow,[1] an American psychologist who died in 1970, created what he called a "Hierarchy of Needs." This psychological theory, in the form of a pyramid, directed that the basic needs of all humans need to be filled in order of importance. Maslow focused on the positive qualities in people and in doing so, developed a new area of scientific study called "humanistic psychology," and his theory came out of his research in this area. As a motivational theory in psychology, in the shape of a pyramid, Maslow stated, "What a man can be, he must be."[2] In other words, people are motivated to achieve certain essential needs, and some take precedence over others. For instance, our most basic need is physical survival, so it will always be the first thing that motivates our behavior.

Once that need is fulfilled, then we can notice, or become motivated by, the next level upward, and so on. Maslow initially stated that individuals must satisfy lower-level deficits before progressing to meet higher level growth needs. However, he later clarified that this satisfaction of primary needs is not an all-or-nothing phenomenon. He admitted that his earlier statements may have given "the false impression that a need must be satisfied 100 percent before the next need emerges."[3] When a deficit need has been more or less satisfied, it eventually will go away. Therefore, our activities become habitually directed toward meeting the next set of needs that we have yet to satisfy, and they become our salient needs. However, growth needs to continue always, and the desire to fulfill our non-essential needs may even become stronger once our primary ones have been engaged, according to Maslow.[4] The need to grow does not stem from a lack of something, but rather, from a desire to grow as a person. Once these growth needs have been reasonably satisfied, one may be able to reach the highest level, called "self-actualization." Every person is capable of moving up the hierarchy to a level of self-actualization, and most people have the desire to do so. Unfortunately, progress is often disrupted by a failure to meet lower-level needs. Difficult life experiences, such as a divorce and loss of a job, may cause an individual to fluctuate between levels of the pyramid. Therefore, not everyone will move through the hierarchy in a unidirectional manner; they may instead move back and forth between different types of needs.

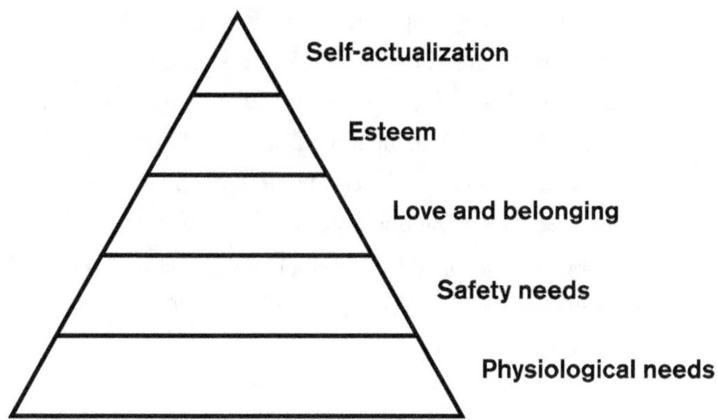



The Original Five-Stage Model of Hierarchy Of Needs Includes:[5]

**Biological and physiological needs:** air, food, drink, shelter, warmth, sex, and sleep.

**Safety needs:** protection from elements, security, order, law, stability, freedom from fear.

**Love and belongingness needs:** friendship, intimacy, trust, and acceptance, giving and receiving affection and love. Also, affiliating with and being part of a group (family, friends, work).

**Esteem** needs, which Maslow classified into two categories: (1) esteem for oneself (dignity, achievement, mastery, and independence) and (2) the desire for reputation or respect from others (e.g., status, prestige). Maslow indicated that the need for respect or reputation is most important for children and adolescents and precedes real self-esteem or dignity.

**Self-actualization needs:** realizing personal potential, self-fulfillment, seeking personal growth and peak experiences, and a desire to become everything one is capable of becoming.

As noted, Maslow suggested that human needs are arranged in a hierarchy. The order of actual needs might be flexible, based on external circumstances or individual differences. For example, he claims that for some individuals, the need for self-esteem is more important than the need for love. For others, the need for creative fulfillment may supersede even the most basic needs. Maslow also points out that most behavior is motivated by multiple needs and says that "any behavior tends to be determined by several or all of the basic needs simultaneously rather than by only one of them."[6] Opposed to Maslow's Hierarchy of Needs is a linear, unidirectional movement model toward happiness. Let's see what Aristotle's theory says about happiness.

**Aristotle's viewpoint**

According to Nicomachean Ethics, Aristotle recognized that happiness operates as a kind of baseline in human life, in the sense that we cannot reasonably ask why we should seek to be happy. It is not a means to something else, as money or power generally are. It is more like wanting to be respected. Desiring it just seems to be part of our nature. Here, then, is a foundational term of sorts. The problem is that the search for happiness is so desperately uncertain. The idea seems both vital and ethereal. What counts as happiness?

Someone who is determined to become an actor may spend fruitless hours auditioning while living on a pittance. For much of the time, they are anxious, dispirited, and mildly hungry—not what we would usually call happy. Their life is not currently pleasant or enjoyable. Yet they are, so to speak, prepared to sacrifice their happiness for their happiness. What if we find it in terrorizing old ladies, or some other activity that society frowns upon? Is there a point where the greater good is more important than our happiness? Happiness is sometimes seen as a state of mind. But this is not how Aristotle regards it. "Well-being," as we usually translate his term for happiness, is what we might call a "state of soul," which for him involves not just an interior condition of being, but a disposition to behave in certain ways. Happiness for Aristotle is attained by virtue, and he feels that virtue is, above all, a social practice rather than an attitude of mind. Happiness is part of a practical way of life, not some private inner contentment. Happiness—or well-being for Aristotle—then involves a creative realization of one's typically human faculties. It is as much something we do, as something we are. And it cannot be done in isolation, which is another way in which happiness differs from the pursuit of pleasure.

**A new model**

By taking Maslow and Aristotle together, we can conceive of another model: that of a triangle, where everything is categorized into the three parts: Health, Wealth, and Worth. You'll see later how each section's importance varies from person to person and can change over one's lifetime, as well. This is, of course, still a simplification of our true needs, but as categorization goes, it's better than trying to fit human complexity into less specific categories. Later, we'll dig a bit deeper into each of the Health, Wealth, and Worth categories to better understand what they are and how they contribute to our happiness. But next we will explore areas where we may have the power to increase our happiness by bringing our life into better alignment with our needs and goals.

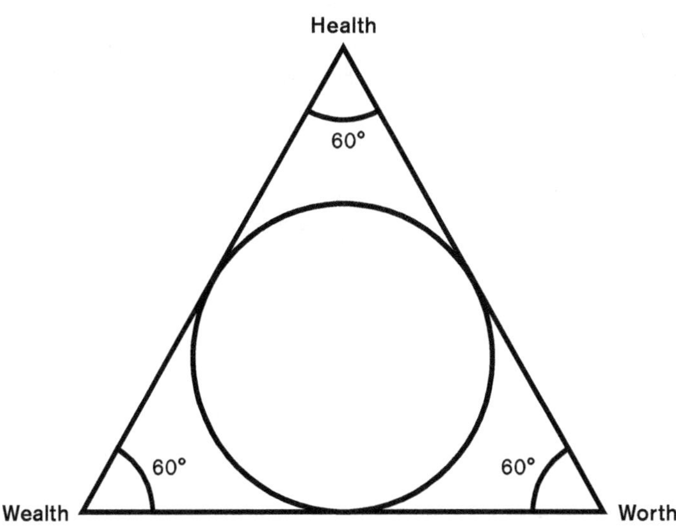

# Chapter 4
**Aligning human needs with our goals**

As we saw in Maslow's pyramid, the biological and physiological needs of a person, along with safety, love, esteem, and self-actualization, are universal among all humanity. What varies from person to person is the specific degree to which we need each of these. That's where things get a bit tricky. Within this concept, there are basic personal goals in life, which I have discovered are to keep ourselves healthy, wealthy, and worthy. The balance that comes between the three elements—or energies that these elements create together—is what I call happiness. This new model of happiness is based on the three life goals of Health, Wealth, and Worth. Fulfilling these needs is essential in achieving sustainable happiness and living a life that we are proud of. The formula is easy to share with the next generation. When I discovered the difference between short-term pleasure, or looking at life through rose-colored glasses, and long-term, true happiness that is sustainable, it changed my life completely. How? Imagine that our ife is defined by the three angles of a triangle as pictured below. The first angle represents the state of our Health, our relationship to our own body and the strength of our well-being. The second angle stands for our Wealth—the state of our personal economy. Our financial status encompasses how we take care of our Wealth and how it takes care of us. The third, Worth, symbolizes the state of our connection to society, and personal relationships with our family and our role within them. It also takes into consideration our contributions and connections.

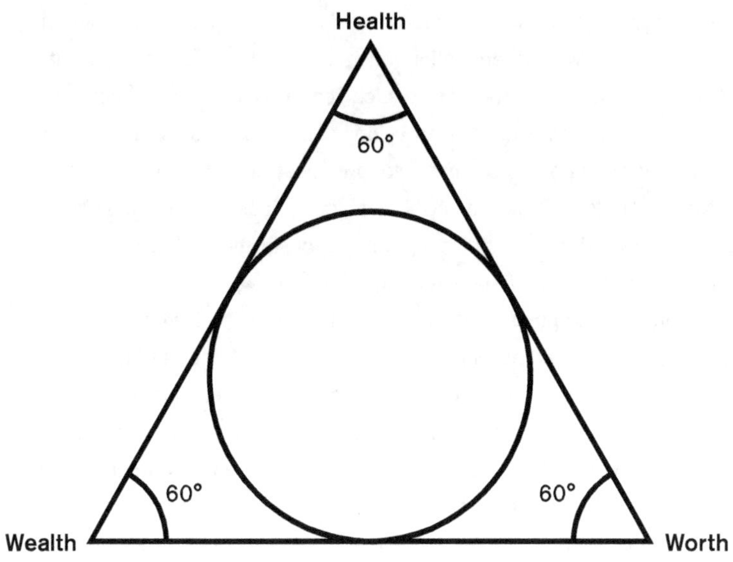



## What is the meaning of these specific angles?

The concept of the 60-degree angle is very important in the understanding of this simple model of happiness. The major trait of an equilateral triangle—balanced and equal on all sides—is that each angle measures 60 degrees. This means that all the three angles sum up to 180 degrees, which, in turn, yields the 180-Degree Rule of Sustainable Happiness model. Since the angles in the triangle above are equal, all the sides of the triangle are equidistant from one another. The goal is to make sure that a balance exists between Wo, We, and H so that an equilibrium level—or maximum level of happiness—can be attained at a point in the middle of the Happiness Triangle (represented by O in the figure above). The closer our angles are to 60 degrees, the more joy we will have and will enjoy a better life. When one of the angles equals zero, we don't have a life at all. When we turn 18 years old, most of us are told that we are on our own and must be responsible of our own happiness and life. However,

no one—not parents, friends, or schools—told us how to prepare to take on
that responsibility. Modern education teaches facts, but not experience. It
is like becoming a parent—there is no such school to attend for experience
on how to be a parent. We just learn by doing. Life teaches us what is right
and wrong, and the people we meet along the way contribute positively or
negatively to our learning. So it is with happiness, too. As times goes by,
we copy others' behaviors, abdicating our responsibilities in life, or for life,
because we have no experience in living.

We ignore our Happiness Triangle—or don't even know it exists—and
focus on one or two angles without conscious consent or understanding
of the consequences. I discovered that these three angles must be
constantly examined, always being checked, cleaned, and updated with
new content. If we fail to do so, we won't be able to keep up with changing
circumstances. We run off to other countries because we think it'll be easier
to fill one of the angles over there, but in actuality, it may be safety, money,
love, or experiences that we're running after. Without realizing it, sometimes
we run after the wrong things. We may not know that we have a Happiness
Triangle, never mind that it needs to be checked regularly. The same way
we check and clean our home so it continues to be fresh and healthy, we
need to check and regularly clean the Wealth, Worth, and Health angles
of our Happiness Triangle. If we don't spot-check our Happiness Triangle,
it becomes cluttered and ineffective, holding us back from fulfilling our
needs and goals. But if we take the time to learn about 180-Degree Rule
of Sustainable Happiness model and look after our angles, we can create
and maintain an equilateral triangle: the perfectly balanced, 60-degree
Happiness Triangle that we are looking for. This method can work for
everyone who is willing to learn it and apply the theory. Would you like
to learn more about what makes up each of these angles?

# Chapter 5
**What are health and wealth?**

**Thoughts about health**

*"You cannot live your life if you don't have it!"* [7]

The supreme goal of humanity is to keep oneself healthy, sustaining 60 degrees of Health, during one's entire life. There are some factors we have limited control over—our natural health, for example—while there are others where we have a great degree of control. Healthy food, freedom from addiction, fitness, and living a low-stress lifestyle are all factors that contribute to happiness and well-being. These are also factors over which we generally have control. More on that later. In order to have a better understanding of the Health (H) angle of the Happiness Triangle, I will divide the definition of "being healthy" into three different components: Physical Health, Psychological Health and Spiritual Health. While it is best that each component is balanced into 20-degree sections (3 multiplied by 20 degrees equals the 60-degree angle of Health), it may be that for people with inescapable health issues, physical health will never be able to equal a full 20 degrees. In that case, or in any other circumstance where one component's full potential is impossible to achieve, the other components must take over to reach a full 60 degrees in the Health angle. And as we age, we must give more thought each section to ensure these three areas remain balanced within the Health angle, or balanced within our circumstances.

1. Physical health
Physical appearance might be thought of as one of the most commonly visible indicators that a person is healthy or unhealthy. Truly, the definition of physical health goes beyond the level of an absence of diseases to the

level of fitness, strength, and energy. Physical health can be evaluated through the following elements: [8]

- Physical activity—includes strength, flexibility, and endurance
- Nutrition and diet—includes nutrient intake, fluid intake, and healthy digestion
- Alcohol and drugs—includes the abstinence from or reduced consumption of these substances
- Medical self-care—includes addressing minor ailments or injuries and seeking emergency care as necessary
- Rest and sleep - includes periodic rest and relaxation, along with high quality sleep

Some people are unfortunately born with chronic illnesses, disabilities, or other disorders that make them ill. In adjusting their components to equal an ideal 60 degrees for Health, they will have different qualities they need to modify than people without these illnesses or disabilities. And as people age, physical health may decline or change and present new problems, or exacerbate those that have been there all along. For a happy life during all our stages of life, we need to make sure that to the best of our circumstances, we are satisfying the first criteria of our Happiness Triangle—Health. As discussed, Maslow spotlighted the basic physiological needs that must be fulfilled in order to survive, such as food, water, and safety. These basic requirements of life are a self-evident aspect of well-being. The odds are, if you're reading this, you are meeting these basic needs.

2. Psychological health

Once we have fulfilled our physical health needs as much as possible according to our circumstances, we may find there are other necessities important for our well-being that we are not successfully satisfying. According to the World Health Organization, psychological health, as well as mental health, is defined as: **A state of well-being in which**

**every individual realizes his or her own potential, can cope with the
normal stresses of life, can work productively and fruitfully, and is able
to make a contribution to her or his community.**[9] The shocking news is
that not everyone who looks healthy physically is sound in mind and spirit.
Some mental health complications result in suicide or extreme unhappiness.
Many use smiles and jokes to cover up their innermost negative feelings.
When asked, "Are you happy?" their answer is often "Yes," but they are
living in denial, not being honest with themselves or others.

They are often those who end up living and dying unhappily, dissatisfied
with life. That is why, if we want to achieve sustainable degrees of
happiness, facing our psychological health challenges must be as
important to us as facing our dreams, or chasing Wealth and Worth. As
people age, those who do not want to face the facts that life is changing
may struggle against these new "normal stresses of life" unnecessarily. Some
reject the idea that they are growing old and try to carry on as they did when
young. Others let themselves become discouraged and depressed, filled with
self-pity or even bitterness. Still others may put themselves on a pedestal
and make demands because of their being old. All such attitudes are most
unwise. Psychological traits such as foolishness and negative emotions
can grow to become obstacles to enjoying life. Introverts may have a harder
time with negativity, potentially lacking a good support system around them.
When young people develop self-control and discipline in their lives, these
traits will follow them all their life and help them make the psychological
adjustments that maturity and aging requires. Those who have taken it easy
on themselves will probably be emotionally ill-equipped to adjust to the
common physical and psychological changes that occur as the years pass.


3. Spiritual health

In the earlier stories regarding my daughter and my mother, I explained how
I first encountered the force that is at work in all our lives. It is the subtle but
barely visible influence of the human spirit, which is illuminating and active
in every human soul. Believe it or not, it is even more active among those
who think they are neither religious nor spiritual. Recognizing and supporting

this spirit requires us to look at the big picture and have an open mind. When people accused Albert Einstein of being atheist, he said, "I am not an atheist… We are in the position of a little child entering a huge library filled with books in many languages… The child only dimly suspects a mysterious order in the arrangement of the books, but doesn't know what it is."[10] I am not asking you to believe in God, or a religion, if you don't want to. But I am asking you to consider Einstein's attitude toward the unknown when considering your spiritual health.

We can see this spirit at work in small children whose eyes light up with joy when they recognize someone they love, or when they are applauded for an achievement. Some of us recognize a certain "aliveness" within when something moves us deeply, or during a moment that touches the heart with a release of joy. Recognizing this spirit is an important step in fulfilling our spiritual health.

## We are all similar, yet different

No matter where or when we live, there is a unique part of us that is the human spirit. It often rises spontaneously and can surprise us by breaking through our defenses, rising from deep within. Exactly where and when we feel permission to cry, laugh out loud, and say "Wow!" is shaped by our personal and cultural history and unique personality. We are profoundly different, yet there still is an undergirding of shared humanity. At the center of that shared humanness there is the profound, animating dynamic of our soul: the human spirit. In the right hands, it can unite, empower, and positively transform people and whole societies.

## Mindfulness supports spiritual health

It is often said that when the mind is troubled, the body is weakened. The state of our mindfulness is a very important element to review when Health issues are concerned:

  • How many times have we been in a situation where we are physically present, but emotionally absent?

• How often do we have to rewind a movie to listen to the dialogue
because even while we were watching it, we were thinking
of something else?
• How often do we have to reread important material because
our distracted brain didn't absorb it properly the first time?

We have all found ourselves in these situations, but do we understand how
they can be a huge shortcoming with regard to our Health? It is a strong
indication that our minds are not in a healthy place. Mindfulness means
maintaining a moment-by-moment awareness of our thoughts, feelings,
bodily sensations, and surrounding environment. Mindfulness also involves
acceptance, meaning that we pay attention to our thoughts and feelings
without judging them. This includes not believing, for instance, that there's
a "right" or "wrong" way to think or feel in a given moment.

When we practice mindfulness, our thoughts tune into what we're
sensing in the present moment, rather than rehashing the past or imagining
the future. Research shows that mindfulness aids spiritual health.[11] The
benefits of practicing mindfulness can include: reduced daydreaming,
stress reduction, boosts to working memory, more focus, less emotional
reactivity, more cognitive flexibility, and increased relationship satisfaction.
Also, mindfulness has been shown to enhance self-insight, morality,
and intuition, and modulate fear—all functions associated with the brain.
Evidence also suggests that mindfulness meditation has numerous health
benefits, including increased immune functioning, improvement to well-being,
and reduction in psychological distress.[12] And if you needed more proof of
its benefits, mindfulness meditation practice appears to increase information
processing speed, as well as decrease the efforts relating to completing
tasks or having thoughts that are unrelated to the task at hand.[13]

## Thoughts about wealth

Many think wealth is a financial abundance of valuable possessions or
money, or a plentiful supply of a particularly desirable thing. If we limit the
definition of wealth to that, it will pertain only to a person with lots of money

and lots of things. Naturally, that definition means that a person who lacks these things is considered poor. I do not agree. Limiting the concept of Wealth to mean ownership of high-value material possessions or cash is understating what Wealth, or being Wealthy, represents. That definition would tempt one to believe that the wealthiest places on Earth are the oil fields of Kuwait or Dubai, or the gold mines of Ghana, etc. This is not the case. Using the 180-Degree Rule of Sustainable Happiness model, generating Wealth begins with our thoughts. It begins with ideas.

How often do we really think? How often do we put our ideas into practice? How often do we procrastinate? The answer to these questions is "too often." We want to begin "someday," instead of choosing a specific day from Monday to Sunday. Few are truly ready to make the adjustments necessary to increase Wealth throughout life, such as learning to cope with a changing lifestyle. They either want the current financial security to remain indefinitely, or for the magical "someday" to occur when they will be financially satisfied forever. This makes graveyards and cemeteries the wealthiest places, because they possess the most untapped potential buried deep down—all the people who have died without sharing their fruits with the planet. The Happiness Triangle's definition of true Wealth, therefore, is something that results from sharing our gifts with all the people on planet Earth. It includes both material and immaterial items, as well as tangible and intangible values. That is why I said because we weren all born with gifts, because everyone has a purpose for which they have been born. No one is a biological accident; everyone is wealthy inside and can be wealthy inside out. In order to have a proper understanding of how the Wealth angle works in this model, we need to subdivide this category into three areas as well: Tangible Wealth (money and possessions), Intangible Wealth, and Time.

1. Tangible wealth
Economists regard money as anything that is generally acceptable as a medium of exchange for goods and services, or for the settlement of debt. For the sake of the 180-Degree Rule of Sustainable Happiness model, money, as a component of Wealth, is taken to mean direct financial reward

for work performed, or in exchange of goods, in the form of cash in hand
and/or in a bank. However, having enough money for just the basics of food
and shelter is not within reach of every person. A fundamental barrier may
be that there is no opportunity to earn enough money.

Perhaps their country has been torn apart by war and there are no jobs,
no fields that can be planted for crops, and no freedom to move to a better
location. The financial definition of "Wealth" is not just having the basics,
but having a great quantity of money or possessions—much more than
one needs. This kind of Wealth is supported by a materialistic attitude
that also includes envy and jealousy. Even people without large financial
means can be materialistic. In a spirit of jealousy, they try to equal or surpass
the economic level of their neighbors, enduring unnecessary pressures of
competition and greed. With poverty abounding, many people have pursued
financial goals to the exclusion of everything else. Some resort to dishonesty
to achieve the financial definition of wealth. Similar to Health, therefore,
each person must examine this component of the Wealth angle in their
personal life. Is it balanced within the scope of our circumstances—what
we have versus what we want? Is our Wealth sufficient, not too little
and not too much?


2. Intangible wealth
Intangible Wealth includes objects and experiences that normally do not cost
any money, like artistic creations, accomplishments, rich experiences, and the
enjoyment of the wonders of nature or the glories of art and performance.
We can use the senses to collect this Wealth into our personal "bank":

- Hearing the sweet melodies of birds or children laughing,
  or a loved one's voice
- Tasting food and experimenting with its growth and preparation
- Watching a beautiful garden grow or the sun set, or seeing
  children growing up healthy
- Smelling a meadow on a hot summer day, or after a midday
  rain; inhaling the fragrance of flowers

- Experiencing laughter and humor
- Feeling a loved one's caress, or participating in sex
- Having personal satisfaction, peace, love, security, and contentment

We may not think that these things are "Wealth," but just try living without them. These activities and experiences, which are generally free of cost, enrich our life and fill us with happiness and joy.

3. Time

It is often said that time is money. What we do with our time is a great factor that determines how wealthy or poor we can become. One of the biggest differences between those who consider themselves successful regarding Wealth and those who are struggling is how they manage and value their 24 hours. Time is a resource that must be regarded as Wealth. The time one takes to perfect a craft must be valued, even when the Wealth within it has yet be converted to cash. This time concept will be expanded in later chapters when we will be looking at the relationship between being busy and being happy, and how time plays a vital role in managing stressful situations that could lead to unhappiness.

# Chapter 6
**What is worth?**

**Thoughts about worth**

The word "Worth" is not used very often in our daily lives. People
define it to mean how much money someone has, the value of something
in terms of money, the value in an individual's ability, or how essential
they are. In this book, Worth means much more than the amount of
cash one has in hand or at the bank. By Worth I mean usefulness or
importance, as to the world, to a person or people, or for a purpose.
It is one's contribution to the world, a philosophy, a group, or an individual.
It begins with the discovery and acknowledgement of the reason for our very
existence, followed by an unceasing desire to accomplish this purpose—not
just for our sake, but for the sake of others. The realization of our Worth
is fueled by a craving not to rob planet Earth of our gifts. To properly
understand this angle, let's again break down the 60-degree angle of
Worth into three subcategories: Purpose, Relationships, and Contribution.

**1. Purpose**

Science still has not discovered exactly why we need meaning in our life,
but there is no arguing that we do. As humans, we feel unfulfilled if we
can't answer the big questions in life, such as "What is my purpose?"
and "What is the meaning of life?" While clear, scientific answers to these
questions remain out of reach, we each, nevertheless, find some peace
with answers of our own. We discover answers that address our meaning
of happiness and purpose, help us understand the world around, and
generate a feeling that we belong to the greater good, including knowing
the reasons for our actions, having self-awareness, raising children, and
developing clear goals and objectives in life. There is nothing more tragic
in life than living without a reason. In his book titled Knowing your Potential,[14]
author Myles Munroe explained that the greatest tragedy in life is not death,
but life without a purpose. It is more tragic to be alive and not know why

than to have died and not known life. Many people die without knowing
why they were born in the first place. Living without a purpose can be
likened to living with an inferior feeling within, such as feeling that we are
a biological accident. Finding our purpose is the greatest discovery that we
can ever make here on Earth. Our purpose was determined before we were
born and it is trapped inside us, but it is our duty to notice it, nourish it, and
make it our own.

Knowing our purpose
Knowing what we are capable of doing, what we can accomplish, or what
we were born to do is one of the most important discoveries of our life. We
can never know our Worth if we don't know what we are capable of doing,
or what we were born to do. Every human being is capable of realizing
and sharing their full value with mankind once they discover it. In fact,
everyone was born to accomplish and share their gifts.

Involvement
As stated in the foreword, to be happy, we must be doing something.
We must be involved in something we love in order to fulfill our goals
in life. We all have to do this, knowing that it's a challenge. Fortunately,
getting involved is easy as long as we are doing something that will lead
to the next step in the challenge.

Are you stuck?
Let me begin by giving you some reasons why you are still where you are,
despite your desire to leave and move on to something greater or better.
Our desires and wants must be matched by dos and don'ts if we want real
results. For instance, it is not enough to desire stopping work as a waitress
and becoming a journalist, like we always dreamed of when we were a kid.
    The fact that we see ourselves broadcasting the news when
we are asleep does not mean that when we wake up next morning, we will
mysteriously have become a journalist. No, when we wake up, we are still
going to be a waitress. But if we do something toward becoming a journalist

while we are awake today, and keep adding to it every day, one day we will
fall asleep a journalist, and not a waitress. The good news is that eventually,
we will fall asleep as a journalist and we will wake up as a journalist. What
does this example mean? Most of the time, we wish to someday become
something that we love. But Someday is not a day of the week. All we
have is Monday to Sunday. Procrastination is one of the biggest killers of
dreams, and the biggest thief of our Worth. So get up, put in the work, enjoy
the journey, and live up to your Worth.

Why you should chase a dream and not money
I will begin this part of the book by sharing a story of man I met in
Sweden, his experience, and how it changed his life. A couple of years
ago I met a man called Victor, a very successful pastor, businessman, and
motivational speaker. Being young and very ambitious and uncertain about
what the future had to offer, I summoned the courage to approach this
man to find out what his secret for success was. He answered my question
with a little story which went as follows: *When I finished high school I was
a very brilliant student both in the Arts and Sciences. At that time there
were many opportunities in the Science field which would fetch so much
money. Many of my friends dove into these and had very good careers.
But when I looked deep down, I realized that [although] I was a good
Science student, I didn't have a passion for it. I always found myself
thinking of business and talking to people. This came more naturally and
easy for me. So I decided to follow this path. This meant that I needed
to study more, and was unemployed for some time, but I did not stop
believing in my dream of becoming an inspiration to others. Today I have
a PhD in Theology, I have many businesses all over the world, and what
my friends earn in one year, I earn in one day. This is because I get paid
for what I know, and not what I do. So I tell you, young man, find what you
love to do and chase it and become it!* After listening to this story, I was
very inspired. We all have the ability to bear fruit—to make a contribution to
the world. The fruits we bear are determined by the Worth we give to them.
These fruits, in turn, provide Worth to us. People are attracted to us because

of our fruit. But we must make sure that we unlock our inner minds first and be honest with ourselves with regard to what we are really capable of doing, what makes us happy while we do it, and what we need to do to be excellent at it. The beauty about doing what you we is that we enjoy the in-between steps we take toward our goals, and not just the final results. This will make us happier and more fulfilled. So, find your purpose, focus on it, and let your fruits clearly display and exhibit your Worth. Shawn Achor, in his book The Happiness Advantage, says that when we work on and do what we love, the money we earn will always be enough and we will be happy. Let us strive to be paid for what we know, rather than what we do.

## 2. Relationships

This refers to the state of being connected to others. Not only to intimate partners, family, and close friends, but also colleagues, associates, and community. Relationships generate many emotions, such as love and lust, passion and compassion, resonance and belonging. We live on a planet full of humans. Sociology tells us that we are all social animals, and in order to live satisfactorily in this global village, we need to live as collective beings and care for one another. We are born to be with others, and relationships play a vital role when it comes to the valuation of our Worth. People in healthy relationships, both at work and out of the workplace, find themselves feeling more worthy and valued and are much happier than people in unhealthy relationships, or without them at all.

The explosion of users on Facebook and Twitter shows how badly people want to be connected to one another, although in some ways, it also illustrates how disconnected people are in real life—so much so that they sit behind a computer and stay glued to the keyboard, chatting all day with people they have never met and may never meet, in order to fulfill this connective fantasy. Relationships can also be defined as staying in touch with family members, nurturing the marriage bond, parents caring for their children, etc. When there is a lack of positive relationships, people often feel less worthy and not accepted by others. This affects happiness negatively, but the opposite is true as well. Good things happen when we are with the right people, at the right time, in the right way. Like magic, we come alive and our world—our capacity to flourish and engage with life, and our happiness—expands. But when we are completely isolated from the right people, everything shrinks. And slowly we die.

## 3. Contribution

How do we bring our gifts to the world? Happiness is found when we are contributing to the world in a way that is meaningful, matters, and allows us to feel that we matter. We feel like we are accessing our full potential, our strengths and our gifts, leaving nothing untapped. Almost every employer asks a potential employee these questions in a recruiting interview, and they are pertinent to our discussion:

- What do you bring to the table for this company?
- Why should we hire you?

Contribution is our fruit. We have our own quota for contributing to the success of any particular venture. Our gifts are what make our presence and our absence noticeable. Every individual who dreams of achieving big things in the future must think about this concept of contributing their gifts. Achieving "big" simply implies that we too are a huge gift to others. Once we turn ourselves into a huge contributor, people will gravitate to us in search of our fruit. That is why sharing our gifts enhances relationships. Many people in the world complain that no one likes them; however, if we look at their way of life critically, we will often find that they do not focus on making contributions. If we focus on the tree, not the fruit, no one will look at our tree once a similar tree pops up and bears much fruit. Contribution calls on us to bear our fruit and share our gifts, attracting people to us.

Success

What is success? This charged word can mean different things to different people. The higher the education that one has received, the more successful many persons hold them to be. Others judge it by laying great importance on material riches as evidence. Receiving positive feedback, especially from people we are involved with in important relationships, feels like success. A person might feel successful after reaching an interim goal—such as a promotion, or a degree in higher education—or when being rewarded in some manner for hard work or achievements. But success isn't money or rewards. Those are simply proxies for accomplishments. Success comes from the feeling and confidence that we are on our way to achieve our goals in life. Success comes from knowing that we are doing things well, learning something new, accomplishing our goals, having a legacy to leave behind, and achieving fame. For our purposes, it is the recognition from others that what we do has value. What does that mean for us? Who judges our success—other people or us? And what is the standard we are judged by?

# Chapter 7
**The 180-degree rule of sustainable happiness model**

The quest for a happy life often seems endless. Even in the Declaration
of Independence of the United States, it is the pursuit of happiness—and
not happiness itself—that is considered an inalienable right. The founders
of the United States who wrote those magnificent words had a very specific
idea. Despite their decision that it was the government's duty to provide
a platform in which every citizen has an opportunity to chase their dreams
(to be healthy and wealthy), the final decision to be happy lies with the
citizens themselves. Many scholars have tried to construct programs that
help people be happy. Some relate to physical training and keeping fit
(sports), psychiatric programs to help those with stress (as well as mental
and emotional problems), and economic programs that may lead people
to wealth and financial independence.

But despite all of this, billions of people around the world are still
unhappy, and many feel unhealthy and poor. Why is this the case? After
years of research and experimentation, I realized that no single program
has all it takes to provide a solution to this problem. The interaction between
Worth, Health, and Wealth is the key, as it takes a combination of the three
parameters to guarantee a full measure of sustainable happiness. When
each of the angles are in total connectivity with each other, there is an
even distribution within the 180 degrees—each 60-degree angle equally
shared. Before I go into a detailed explanation of how the 180-Degree
Rule of Sustainable Happiness model works, I would like to point out that
this model is not rocket science. It is very easy to understand, and anyone
around the world can apply it. The beauty of it is that it does not discriminate
with regard to gender, race, age, profession, or religion. Whoever and
wherever we are, so long as we are a citizen of planet Earth, we will
find this model useful.

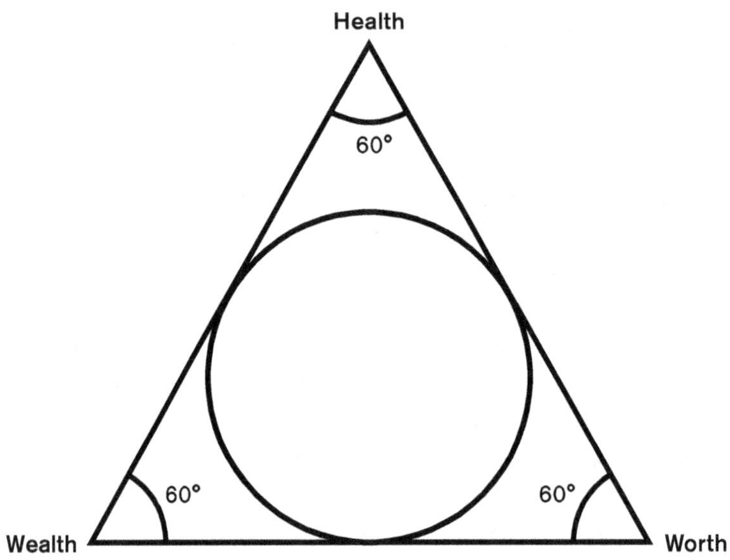


As mentioned earlier, the 180 degrees are divided equally into three parts of three angles of 60 degrees. At the base of the triangles we have 120 degrees representing Worth (Wo) and Wealth (We) respectively. At the peak we have an angle also equal to 60 degrees representing Health (H). The figure above shows the interrelatedness of these three parameters (Wo, We, and H). None is independent of the other.

### Relationship between worth and wealth

If you recall in my explanation of the meaning of Worth (Wo), I explained why it is important to chase a dream and not money. But that does not cancel out the fact that Worth and Wealth (We) have a very strong relationship. This connection can best be seen when one examines the relationship between flowers and bees. When a plant is still very young, without any flowers, few bees fly to it. But when the same plant produces flowers, it attracts bees to itself for mutual benefits. Another example is the relationship between humans and a fruit tree. It takes a fruit tree, such as a mango tree, many years to grow. Before then, how often do people climb up it just for the sake of it? Not so often…besides children, maybe none at all. But once a mango tree bears fruit, many people climb it to pluck some mangoes. The motto is: Our fruit is what attracts others. There are people who complain that people dislike them, how life is so unpleasant, how no one cares. They need to learn how to bear fruit and people will come to them. Wealth is the feedback of what we get from others, as well as what we get from our inner self and the fruits and gifts we share with the world. The relationship between Wo and We is very simple. The fruit that comes from Wo receives a reward from those who value these gifts, adding to We. We are happier and wealthier when we chase our dreams, because We is attracted by our fruit. But assuming that we have pursued our dreams and borne fruit and become wealthy, does that mean we will have achieved happiness? Should we just fold our arms and enjoy our Wealth? The answer is no. That would be a highway to unhappiness because within this straightforward 180-Degree Rule of Sustainable Happiness model, happiness is not and will not be determined by a simple, single parameter.

Relying on only one angle can lead to ruin
To fully understand this, consider the following story regarding the relationship between We and Wo. While growing up in a small village in Africa, I had a very humble family background. As a young ambitious student, I tried to get close to rich people to see how they lived. I thought that if I could discover how they had become rich, I could copy their methods and also become prosperous. That was my goal at the time. But there was one thing that I could not understand. One very rich man didn't seem to be very happy at all. How could a rich person with so much money and assets be unhappy? He could buy lots of things with his money that would make his life entertaining and exciting. But why is this man unhappy? I kept wondering. Has he been diagnosed with a chronic ailment that is about to take his life? Does he have other health problems? I quietly researched him and found out that he did have some health issues related to psychological problems.

But how can he have mental problems with all that money? What is
he worried about? Many years later, when I was just entering university,
I decided to have a conversation with him to find out what the problem
was. I discovered that his health problems were caused by his abuse of
his success. He used to be a great music composer and artist and worked
on his craft diligently, becoming an expert in his profession. Coming from
a humble background, he had never seen or experienced so much success.
Because people loved his music (his fruit), he had positive feedback and
became very wealthy, since his Worth was worth it (his Wo was worth his
We). Unfortunately, when he became very successful, he stopped putting
time and work into his craft. To him, he had "made it."

He thought that he could use his money to buy anything he wanted.
He decided to accumulate all the luxuries he desired, have the best
doctors to take care of his health, send money to the poor, etc. But
something unexpected happened. His fans stopped reacting positively
to his music and he started losing fans—just like when a tree stops
bearing fruit, no one goes to it. In a quest for alternative sources of fun
and excitement, he began going to clubs and drinking excessively, and got
involved with drugs. That was the beginning of the end. By the time I spoke
to him, he was wishing that he could turn back the hands of time. He had
not managed his Wealth in a responsible or positive manner, and his Wo
and future We suffered greatly. Handling We maturely depends on the
attention we give to Wo, both before and even after we have gotten
We. To accomplish this, we need to strive for a sustainable measure of
happiness through the 180-Degree Rule of Sustainable Happiness model.

**The relationship between worth and health**

This association is very easy to establish. If the true fulfillment of our
potential comes from doing what we love, then that means our Wo (Worth)
relates to our H (Health). Remember earlier when I mentioned enjoying the
"in between" of what we chase and what we love? Having this attitude will
save us from all kinds of unhealthy anxieties that could be detrimental to
our H. Also, our fruits enhance our relationships with others and keep us

healthy from the inside out. And even more, chasing our dreams is fulfilling, fun, and exciting, which helps one stay away from other unhealthy forms of excitement that could be very detrimental to our H. Relating H to Wo is easy in other ways as well. H provides soundness of body and mind, which allows us to pursue our dreams, achieve them, and become worthy to society. Without the right H requirements, our creativity and our ability to achieve the full measure of our potential is impaired. The role H plays on our Wo cannot be overemphasized.

## Relationship between health and wealth

A popular saying from health practitioners is "Health is wealth." The relationship between H and We can be better understood by, first of all, reminding ourselves that We is not measured just by money, but so much more. It is a combination of having enough money for one's needs, having the ability to enjoy that money, being an active contributor to people that society will look up to, being able to have and sustain a meaningful network of friends and family that contributes to wholesome experiences, etc. It includes the ability of a person to function as a happy, effective individual who is able to make decisions out of a sense of freedom, rather than compulsion. After all, healthy people can work longer and harder than sick people. Healthier children are likely to stay in school longer and learn and earn more when they enter the workforce. Even across countries, the relationship is clear: those with better health are generally richer, and those countries that improve their citizens' health grow faster.

The more we understand what We is, the healthier we become. The illusion that lies behind money sometimes puts forth the idea that a lack of money can be very detrimental to our H. People who regard We to mean just "cash" can feel poor when they lack it. An understanding of the word "Wealth," in both real and insignificant terms, will allow us to see the bigger picture. Everyone with a dream who puts in the work day by day to achieve a dream is wealthy, even if that We has not yet been converted to cash. Faith about our future is fueled by a sense of purpose. This is really what will make us feel wealthy and positively affect our H.

# Chapter 8

**Being busy and being happy**

A common adage says that "an idle mind is the Devil's workshop." It goes without saying that one could not possibly be happy in such a workshop, since the Devil is associated with evil, misery, pain, heartache, etc. But does this mean that being busy is a guarantee to happiness? Can everyone who is busy boast a full measure of happiness? Many researchers have attempted to answer this tricky question. While a lot of scientists feel that happiness has a direct relationship with being busy, others frown at such a generalization. Imagine being busy all day in a workplace that you dislike, stuck at a job where you feel trapped. How can you ever be happy in such a situation? You can't wait for Friday to come or for the clock to hit 5 p.m. (closing time). And Sunday can't be enjoyed because of the dread of the Monday to follow. This type of employment status cannot provide a full measure of happiness because it is bad for our Health and it is bad for our Worth. We are there just because of Wealth. This increases the angle of We, but at the same time increases the distance between Wo and H.

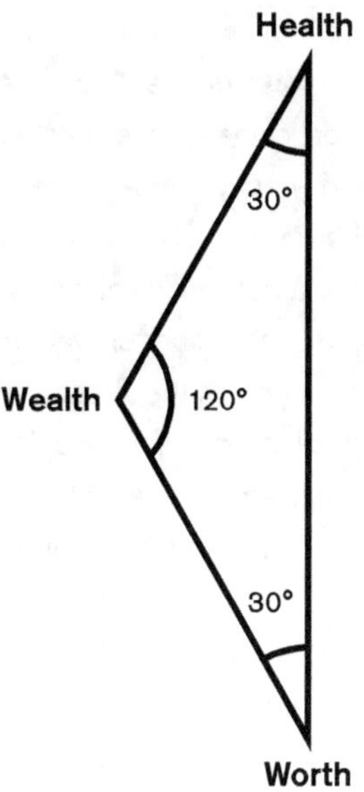


In the figure above, we can clearly see what happens to Wo and H
when too much attention is given to We. This is an example of a person
who is busy but not happy. They are just working just for money. Their hard
work might increase their We angle, but at the same time it reduces the Wo
and H angles. The inappropriate focus on We also increases the distance
between Wo and H, thus shifting the Happiness Triangle away from
balance. A similar analogy holds true if the focus is on Wo or H. Being
busy has a maximum positive effect on happiness when the person who
is busy is not being rushed, and when the consequences of being busy
do not influence either of the other two angles to their detriment.

How stress affects our Happiness Triangle
Let us take the game of football, for example. When the opposing
side scores the first goal at the 10th minute in the first half of the game,
the players of the other team will continue to play very well. They will keep

their cool and maintain better control of the ball—all because they are aware that they still have 80 minutes to make up the difference. But the mentality changes drastically when this goal comes at the 80th minute of the game. The resulting stress, anxiety, and worry will reduce their skill. This simple analogy depicts the fact that the same levels of work stress can be perceived differently, and it can affect the level of happiness in different angles. When humans feel like they have control over time in stressful situations, their creativity is enhanced and the stress appears to be less, or less important—unlike in situations when people feel rushed and perceive stress to be uncontrollable and inescapable. While doing nothing can be the biggest cause of depression and unhappiness, being busy needs to be qualified with control over stress and time, especially if it is to yield the full measure of happiness in relation to being busy. This scenario is demonstrated in the figure on the next page.

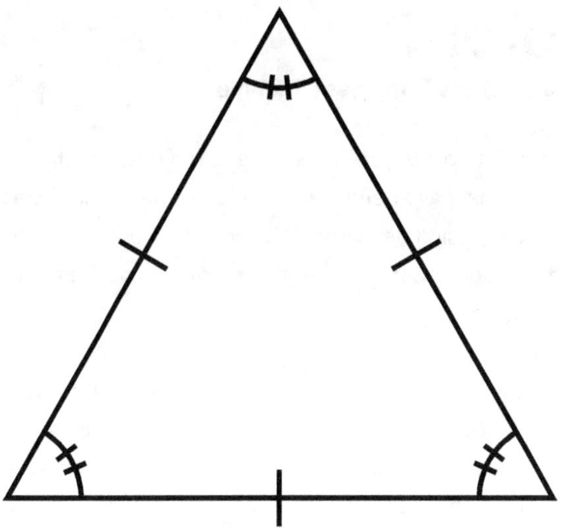

**Equilateral triangle**

This equilateral Happiness Triangle is similar to the one used previously
to demonstrate the concept of a sustainable equilibrium level of happiness.
When people feel they have time on their hands and are not being pushed,
the situation gives them room to keep fit and stay healthy, focus on and
enhance their productivity, and hence, increase their Wealth. This equilateral
model is somewhat hypothetical; it is not something that can be achieved
in a day, but it is worth striving for if we want to be happy.

# Chapter 9
**The three rules of the Happiness Triangle**

These rules will disturb everyone's Happiness Triangle, and they are the reasons why we must pay attention to our triangle and angles, clearing out the clutter and refocusing on our goals. If we don't, our Happiness Triangle will stay cluttered and become ineffective, holding us back from fulfilling our needs and goals.

1. The angles will change because they represent our everyday growth: "Day, the glorious light of the creator, is beloved of men and women, a source of hope and happiness to rich and poor, and of service to all."[15]
2. If one angle changes, it automatically affects the other angles.
3. The angles don't lie.

We live in a constantly moving world where we are continuously growing. The goal is to keep moving and growing by keeping all the angles at 60 degrees every day. By accomplishing that, we can live a happy life forever. So why don't we do that?

**What is the challenge?**
Many people in the world focus on the wrong issues instead of paying attention to the issues represented by the three angles in the 180-Degree Rule of Sustainable Happiness model. Then again, some only focus on one angle at a time, thinking that is good to have a nice body and feel good and forgetting to work on their Wealth or Worth angles. Others spend their time helping others to the point that they forget to take care of their own Health or Wealth angles. Meanwhile, there are some whose sole objective is making money. They wake up and go to work every day, chasing money, and forget that the Health and Worth angles need to have the same amount of time spent on them as the "chasing money" angle, Wealth. By spending varying amounts of time on the three angles and their

sub-angles, human beings can create different Happiness Triangles that will yield different lifestyle results.

**Models of Happiness Triangles**

On the next page there are some models of other Happiness Triangles that exemplify this concept. The names below each symbol in the first drawing are the correct geometric designations, which is where our Happiness Triangles get their names:

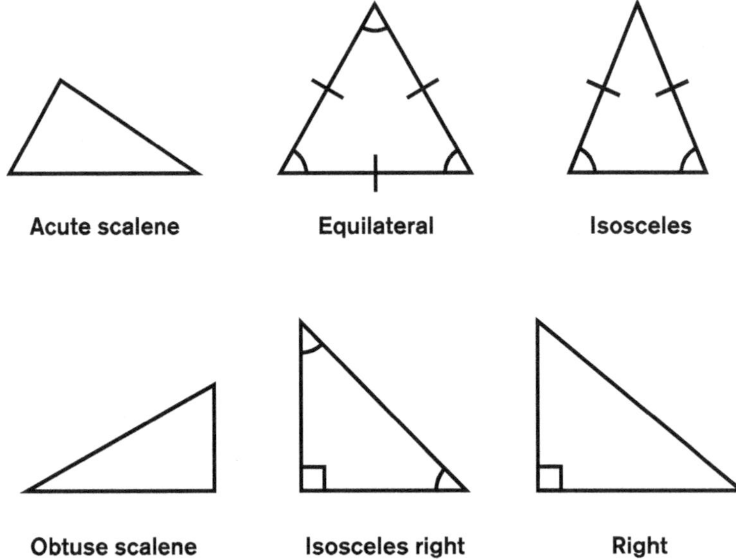



A person has **"Acute Happiness"** when all three of the Happiness Triangles angles are acute. If, for instance, the Health angle is larger than 90 degrees, we have not reached a balance. A person has an **"Obtuse Happiness"** situation when his Worth angle is larger than 90 degrees.

A **"Right Happiness"** triangle occurs when one of the angles is equal to 90 degrees. An **"Equilateral Happiness"** or "Perfect Happiness" triangle is in effect when all of the triangle's sides are an equal 60 degrees. A person is having an **"Isosceles Happiness"** when they have two of the angles equal. **"Scalene Happiness"** occurs when all of the triangle's angles are different. A person can also have a triangle that is simultaneously right and isosceles—an **"Isosceles Right Happiness"** triangle.

**What about you?**

Take some time to consider your current situation in light of the material in this book. Review the smaller components of each 60-degree angle and assign numerical scores to each below.

**Calculating your angles**

For each angle, you need to decide what the current state of your angle is. Read the questions below, as they will help you define your current levels.

**Health** = 3 sections of 20 degrees each is optimal

Let's calculate the Health angle. At this moment in time, how satisfied am I with my current level of physical ability, energy, appearance and well-being? What about my ability to weather adversity, and my capacity to feel calm, aware, present, in charge, optimistic and hopeful?

a) Choose a number from 1 to 20. Consider that 20 means you are very satisfied with your physical health, and 1 means you are not satisfied at all.
1 2 3 4 5 6 7 8 9 10 11 12 13 14 15 16 17 18 19 20

b) Choose another number from 1 to 20, with 20 being extremely satisfied with your psychological health, and 1 being completely dissatisfied.
1 2 3 4 5 6 7 8 9 10 11 12 13 14 15 16 17 18 19 20

c) Choose a third number from 1 to 20, with 20 meaning you are very satisfied with the spiritual health level you have now, and 1 meaning you are very dissatisfied.
1 2 3 4 5 6 7 8 9 10 11 12 13 14 15 16 17 18 19 20

Total Score (Degree): A + B + C = Health angle degree

**Wealth** = 3 sections of 20 degrees each is optimal

Let's calculate the Wealth angle. At this moment, how satisfied am I with my economic situation? Am I satisfied with my actions regarding time management? When it comes to the returns from my investments or my spending, am I satisfied with the results?

a) Choose a number from 1 to 20. Consider that 20 is being very satisfied with how much tangible wealth you have, and 1 is very dissatisfied.
1 2 3 4 5 6 7 8 9 10 11 12 13 14 15 16 17 18 19 20

b) Choose a second number from 1 to 20. In this case, 20 means you are completely satisfied with the amount of intangible wealth you have, and 1 means you are terribly dissatisfied.
1 2 3 4 5 6 7 8 9 10 11 12 13 14 15 16 17 18 19 20

c) Choose a third number from 1 to 20. In this case, consider that 20 means you are very satisfied with how you manage your time, and 1 means you are completely dissatisfied.
1 2 3 4 5 6 7 8 9 10 11 12 13 14 15 16 17 18 19 20

Total Score (Degree): A + B + C = Wealth angle degree

**Worth** = 3 sections of 20 degrees each is optimal

Let's calculate the Worth angle. What is the state of my current Worth angle? Right now, how satisfied am I with the depth and quality of loving relationships and friendships? Do I sense genuine belonging coming from bringing my gifts to the world? Do I feel that my gifts are helping others?

a) Choose a number from 1 to 20. Consider that 20 means you are satisfied with your purpose in life, or your path to its discovery, and 1 means you are dissatisfied.
1 2 3 4 5 6 7 8 9 10 11 12 13 14 15 16 17 18 19 20

b) Choose a second number from 1 to 20, with 20 meaning you
are thoroughly satisfied with the quantity and quality of relationships
you have, and 1 means you are terribly dissatisfied.
1 2 3 4 5 6 7 8 9 10 11 12 13 14 15 16 17 18 19 20

c) Choose a third number from 1 to 20. In this case, 20 means
you are completely satisfied with the contributions you are making,
and 1 means you are thoroughly dissatisfied.
1 2 3 4 5 6 7 8 9 10 11 12 13 14 15 16 17 18 19 20

Total Score (Degree): A + B + C = Worth angle degree

Using the degrees you calculated above, use the formula[16]
below to draw your Happiness Triangle to the best of your ability.

Health (SCORE) + Wealth (SCORE) + Worth (SCORE) = Y
Once Y is determined, you can calculate each angle:

Health angle = (180/Y) x Health (SCORE)
Wealth angle = (180/Y) x Wealth (SCORE)
Worth angle = (180/Y) x Worth (SCORE)

Now, which of the different Happiness Triangles shown at the beginning
of the chapter does yours most closely match? Do you see any adjustments
that need to be made?

My Happiness Triangle drawing

# Chapter 10
**Three guidelines for an equilateral Happiness Triangle**

**Guideline 1: Have both commitment and belief**

Commitment to change
If you approach this theory halfheartedly—the task of making changes in your
Happiness Triangle angles so they are more closely equal—it will not work.
You need to take full responsibility and make a commitment to yourself that
you will make things happen. Not your government, family, or society—you.

Believe that you can change
You must jump into your transformation toward happiness with both feet.
It is not a belief in the theory that you need, but rather the conviction that
you can make the change. This belief in yourself comes when you make
a full commitment to change. This theory will inevitably change the world
that you live in, so you need to be prepared ahead of time to adjust to new
situations and circumstances. But you can't change everything at once. For
this new world to be stable, it must be created with simple little baby steps.

How to change
Any drastic change will be unstable or traumatic. Both situations may
derail your efforts in achieving any of the goals (Health, Worth, and Wealth)
you have set for yourself. If your new reality is unstable, you will find yourself
back in the same rut you were in before. Your former rut is familiar, easy,
and attractive. But if you return to it, in fact you may end up deeper
in it, and you will face a new problem: doubt that you can change.
You may even unintentionally develop new stumbling blocks to reaching
your goal of an equilateral Happiness Triangle. A change in a person's
life is actually a death—the death of the old you and preparation for the
new you. If there is no chance to reconcile, reassure, and possibly forgive
your old self, the transformed self will be no different than a repression

of your old self. When there is repression, there is always a reemergence.
For this reason, transformation in small steps is required. Another purpose
of taking it slow is so you can plan out and prepare yourself for your new
life. It is by these small, confident steps that you will create the catalyst
of your happiness.

**Guideline 2: Be positive and curious**

*"The power of positive thinking is like a car with a powerful engine that
can take you to the summit of a mountain."*[17]

What does being positive mean?
It means that you should expect the best to happen in your life. Being
positive is a habit of believing that things will turn out well and not
allowing negative thoughts and doubts to disturb this conviction, even
if your Happiness Triangle doesn't look the way you want it to right now!
Be positive and strive to stay that way. Knowing that you can make changes
is the key to starting the journey to build your equilateral Happiness Triangle.

Constructive thinking
With regard to positivity, when you need solutions, you think of them
and believe that you can find them. Active problem-solving is a must.
It is not enough just to believe that things will turn out okay. You also need
to be vigorous in meditating on constructive solutions and carrying them out.

Creative thinking
When you are looking at life and your circumstances with a broader vision,
you will find creative solutions. With a positive attitude, you will not be afraid
to look for new ways of doing things. This makes you unique, and can make
you more efficient and effective than other people.

Essential life energies
When you are positive in whatever you do, you create three energies
that help you to carry your goals forward:

1. Optimism: This mental attitude is the main characteristic
of being positive. Hope occurs when you are sure your situations
and circumstances will improve. Creative thinking builds optimism
because you will easily see potential problems and make changes
to avoid them. Your plans will turn out well.

2. Motivation: This is the energy and zest to accomplish tasks and
move forward toward your goals. When you are motivated, it is easier
to actively identify goals to work toward. Spending energy and time
on work, studies, or accomplishing a goal will not feel like a burden
or a chore. When you are sure of yourself, believe in your abilities,
and do not allow anything to discourage you, you become motivated.

3. Happiness: A person with a positive attitude is usually happy
and content. When you are positive, you experience pleasant and
happy feelings. This brings brightness to your eyes, more energy
in your body, and happiness. Your whole being broadcasts good
will, happiness, and success. Even your Health will be affected in
a beneficial way. You will "walk tall," your voice will be more powerful,
and your body language will shows the way you feel.

A positive way of life
Adopting a positive attitude as a way of life will help you cope more easily
with your daily affairs and will bring constructive changes into your life.
A positive attitude will make you an optimist, and will help you avoid worries
and negative thoughts. Developing this attitude can make you a happier
person—someone who sees the bright side of life and expects the best
to happen. It is certainly a state of mind that is well worth developing.

A curious approach to life
Curiosity is the desire to learn, to understand new things, and to know how they work. Curiosity can manifest itself in many ways, such as the desire to read the gossip columns or watch a favorite show, or as the desire to learn about people and their lives. It can also manifest as the desire to accumulate knowledge in the fields of science, geography, or other topics, or as the urge to learn how to repair objects or machinery. Curiosity is the expression of the urge to learn and acquire facts and knowledge. It widens the mind and opens it to different opinions, different lifestyles, and different topics. Curious people ask questions, read, and explore.

They actively seek information or experience and are willing to meet any challenges to broadening their horizons. They are not shy, asking questions freely, and delve deeply into whatever topic interests them. Curiosity can be directed to gossip and unimportant details, or to matters that are more important. While learning and acquiring knowledge, it can lead to becoming an expert in one's field. Curiosity is a vital ingredient for becoming a good journalist, writer, inventor, scientist, or any number of other career paths.

Why positivity and curiosity are important
The minds of curious people are active. They want to know and to understand, and they are always positive regarding their work. This puts them in a good position to learn a job and do it better and more creatively, and they are happy doing it. A person who lacks curiosity and is negative will not succeed. When curious people fail, they frequently don't consider it a failure. They analyze the malfunction or problem because they are keen on knowing the reasons why it happened. In doing so, they have confidence that their performance will improve next time. This increases their chances for happiness and success. Being curious is important for excelling in almost any type of job and improving your performance because you ask questions, learn from others, and look for ways to do your job better. If you show more interest in what you are doing, you indicate that you care and wish to learn and progress.

*"When curiosity is alive, we are attracted to many things; we discover many worlds."* [18]

By their nature, children are curious about everything. As a parent, you need to encourage them to ask questions, learn new things, read books, have hobbies, and keep the flame of their curiosity alive. Intellectual curiosity is also an important part of the learning process at every age. Its possession awakens interest, encourages motivation, results in a feeling of being alive, and keeps your mind sharp and agile. Living without curiosity makes life boring, while its presence will ensure a person is more alive and energetic. It keeps the mind strong and in good shape. It stimulates the mind and keeps you young.

*"There are no foolish questions, and no man becomes a fool until he has stopped asking questions."* [19]

A positive, curious mind leads to happiness and success and can change your whole life. If you stay positive, your whole life becomes filled with light. This light affects not only you and the way you look at the world, but also your environment and the people around you. Creating an equilateral Happiness Triangle will become easier.

**Guideline 3: Take responsibility**
This is a main law of life. It is often overlooked, but it is important in your life and a significant key to creating your Happiness Triangle. Taking responsibility comes from self-confidence, or self-love. How much do you like yourself or love yourself? Do you accept yourself as a human being who possesses value? To achieve such a high station, it requires a sense of duty. To assume accountability for yourself means that it is you who decides your destiny—everything you are and everything you will become. There is no other person who can do that. Many people believe in a higher power and may say that the responsibility for life lies with the higher power of God, but God helps the one who helps themselves. You decide

your life yourself. You decide what will happen to you. If you don't like
what is happening, then it is up to you to make sure that it changes.
You cannot give someone else that accountability. It is yours, and that
is an inescapable law of the Universe that directly impacts your Happiness
Triangle. Nowadays, this responsibility is often twisted. Society, or the
government, sometimes thinks that it can make decisions for you, and
that it knows what is good for you. For some people, it leads them in
the direction of allowing society, or the government, to take charge.
For example, if someone commits a crime and ends up in prison, most
of the time a criminal will not accept responsibility for their action.
They blame others, or try to explain why they committed the crime
in the first place. They seem incapable of saying, "Yes, I did that.
I accept the consequences."

A person must understand the laws that govern ourUniverse to
be able to fully reach their potential. You start as a baby and become
mature around 18 years old. In the beginning, as an infant, you have zero
accountability for your life. Generally, as children grow, they are given more
obligations to handle, but this is becoming uncommon as parents and
teachers rely on society or the government. When a child becomes an adult
at age 18, they are legally, psychologically, morally, emotionally, and physically
ready to take over for their own life. Fundamentally, however, it does not
matter if your parents prepared you to shoulder that duty or not. At the
age 18, you are 100% responsible for the rest of your life. You cannot give
away that obligation or revoke it. For your whole life, you are responsible
for all that happens to you or with you. No excuses.

**Change or complain?**

If you don't like the way things are in your life, then it is up to you to make
a change. If you choose not to change, you lose the right to complain and
need to just accept it. A responsible person doesn't complain about their
challenges. They accept everything they encounter in their life, either
making changes to improve or saying nothing about them. For myself,
I know that everything that happens to me depends on me. This can be

a most difficult concept to understand. When adults assume this responsibility and take command, it is easy to fall back into the childhood mode, where they depend on others. They are always looking for what I call the "Kid's Security Zone." In this zone, someone was always taking care of them, and nothing else worried them. In school, they were taken care of. At workplaces, they were taken care of. Do you want to be taken care of all your life, or do you want to be in total control of your life? The responsibility will be yours no matter what you decide. But the choice is up to you.

# Chapter 11
**Individual growth**

Strongly related to Guideline #3 in Chapter 10 is individual growth, but unlike taking responsibility—which happens whether we want it or not—we have a choice to engage in personal growth. Stagnation in individual growth will result in severe distortions in our Happiness Triangle and should be avoided at all costs. Some people seem to feel that because someone else took care of all their needs while they grew up, those people will continue to take care of them after they finish their education. If no one does so, then the individual's life stagnates—nothing happens. In the Chapter 3 discussion of Maslow's Hierarchy of Needs, we saw that self-actualization needs are at the top of the pyramid. Individual growth is part of becoming self-actualized, along with realizing our personal potential and desiring to become everything we are capable of becoming. Choosing to pursue personal growth is the difference between being mature and being immature.

**The road to maturity**

Imagine that there is a road stretching out from being a child to becoming an adult, and everyone will come to the end of that road sooner or later. There they will find a large river that they must cross, and they will need to jump in the water to do so. But will they? One side of the road—the one they're currently on—is Immature Road, and the other side is Mature Road. When we're on Immature Road, we turn to others for solutions, help, and support. We are dependent on others. On the other side of the river is Mature Road. Over there, everyone must make their own decisions. When the road ends at the river, everyone must decide to jump, and the only jump is to AdultLand. At this point, we are transitioning from childhood to adulthood. Sometimes this happens easily as a part of normal development, but sometimes a person has to be forced into the water. Everyone must learn that we make decisions over our life. We are our own architects. What happens next? Wise people who are interested in personal growth are eager to cross the river and start their journey along Mature Road. Unfortunately, some people slosh their way back to Immature Road and look for someone to give them a hand. They want a job where they can avoid responsibility—where a manager will have ultimate accountability for their performance. Sadly, people look for excuses to run away from others, people, or situations. As mentioned in the previous chapter, such people don't have a sense of responsibility, nor do they have an interest in growing as a person. Sometimes people decide to stretch themselves a little and tentatively dip a toe back into the river, but such a hesitant attempt is like adding a drop of water to the ocean. At the first sign of resistance, they come up with excuses to back out of the river. Instead of making an effort to improve, they decide to stay where they are.

Excuses de jour
Making excuses is a disease! It is becoming more and more common to justify our shortcomings, our faults, things we neglected to do, relationships we backed out of, etc. Pretexts and defenses keep us from making even one step forward. Ask yourself: What excuses do I make to defend not taking a step forward? What excuses do I use to ignore my happiness? What's the biggest excuse that comes to mind when you think about something you could do or become? A new job, a new house, new challenges, or new opportunities that could change what you don't like in your life at the moment. What are your excuses?

- I cannot because…
- I should have, but…
- I'll start after (insert event)…
- It's really not that important…
- I could have, except…
- I get by just fine when I (insert action)…
- If I only had the time to…
- I'm too young/old to…

- It's too much work/too much money…
- Yes, but…

If a person tries hard enough, there is always a reason: "I am so young,
I am too old, too big, to small, too long, too short, too little educated,
too much educated, the timing is wrong," etc. Consider the following
questions seriously:

- What are your biggest excuses?
- What is in your brain that defends your excuses?
- What causes you to avoid responsibility?
- What still holds you in, or brings you back to, childhood
on Immature Road?

When we consider personal growth in relation to the Happiness Triangle,
we must also discuss something else for a second time.

Responsibility
As discussed in Guideline #3 in the last chapter, we cannot choose to take
responsibility or not, or just accept a little here or there. It doesn't work like
that. From 18 years old until the end of our life, we are required to be 100%
accountable for our life. We can decide not to use our full potential or take
advantage of opportunities, along with other choices in our life. But with
those decisions comes the obligation to deal with the consequences. If we
want to become what we are capable of, we must take total responsibility for
our Happiness Triangle. We will need to make changes in its angles, as well
as make necessary and complicated decisions. Life is a series of challenges
and obstacles to jump over.

Balance
To achieve an equilateral Happiness Triangle, balance between our needs
and our goals must be created. To accomplish that task, we need a plan
that clearly shows our top unfulfilled goals and how much is left to be

fulfilled. We must understand where our happiness comes from and where it disappears to. This is another 100% responsibility that we cannot give away to someone else.

# Chapter 12

**Conclusion**

Happiness won't come while you sit around and wish for it. I won't fool you by saying that achieving full and complete happiness is easy—it's not. Like everything in life, happiness is something you have to learn how to get and work for. But can you imagine anything else more worthwhile than working on what satisfies and fulfills you most in line with your happiness? A good and happy life is made up of a series of good days, starting with today. Your job is not so much to go from here to there, but to wake up, to own your current reality, to see it, feel it, and accept it. Then you can take action to start living the life you dream of living, one breath, one step, one day at time. Not later, not tomorrow, but today and right now. Today is the glorious light we have been given; it is beloved of men and women, a source of hope and happiness to rich and poor, and of service to all.

All these details lead to today's transformation energy. It is the energy of the 180-Degree Rule of Sustainable Happiness model that will create your sustainable Happiness Triangle. As the day transforms itself into night and night into the light, so can you also. You can rise from the darkness of your life and turn into the light of happiness. Today, this energy has great uses as a changer of ways. But not the usual, common changes that come from year to year, or life to life. Instead, it is a step-by-step transformation. If you are looking to transform your life—such as by losing weight, earning more money, or learning a new skill—the changes must not be made all at once. If one loses a lot of weight quickly, they tend to gain it back because the person hasn't really made a lifestyle change. This lifestyle change can only come one day at time. That's why to build your own equilateral Happiness Triangle, you have to do it by small steps, one day at time. Examine each angle and notice which is in most dire need of filling. Focus your energy on filling the angle that seems to be causing you the most immediate pain. If all the angles appear to need attention equally, then rotate around, filling a different one a little bit each day. Your quest

is to come to a place where your angles are all equal at 60 degrees.
With a functioning equilateral Happiness Triangle, you are moving
through each day feeling vital, energized, strong, alive, and at ease.
You are contributing meaningfully to the world; leveraging your strengths,
values, wisdom, and abilities to their fullest; spending time only on what
truly matters. You are surrounded by people you love being with, embraced
by love and having a deep sense of understanding and belonging. You feel
connected to people and to your spiritual source, however you define it. If you
really want to change yourself, treat this book as your guide and read it in the
order that makes sense for you. Be curious to learn what makes your angles
big or small, and what all those things mean to you. Continue to measure
your Happiness Triangle angles and keep aligning your actions with your
now deeper understanding of who you are and what you most need.

Consider taking a Happiness Triangle snapshot once a day, once
a week, or once a month. Why? It will give you a new baseline to help you
better understand where to focus your energies moving forward. It will
also show you how far you have come when you compare it to your original
Happiness Triangle. Maybe you started with the Wealth angle, but after
working hard to meet a huge deadline and having nonexistent self-care,
that angle of Health is getting smaller. You might not notice it at first, but
a weekly or monthly snapshot will help you see exactly where you are so you
know where to go. The truth is that filling your angles and living a truly happy
life is a constantly moving target. There is no single day when you get to
say, "I have made it! I don't have to do anything more!" There is no finishing
goalpost. Small corrections will be needed to fill your Happiness Triangle
angles until the day you leave this planet. Sustainable happiness is not
a place at which you arrive. It is like a pair of sunglasses through which
you can see and create your world. The question is, will you choose to
create the sustainable happiness that you dream of having? If not now,
when? At the end of your life, you don't want to hear:

−I wish I hadn't taken life so seriously…
−I wish I had lived more…
−I wish I had more happiness with my family…
−I wish I had known how precious life is…
−I wish I hadn't given up on my dream so easily…

Because, one day your life will flash before your eyes. Make sure it's worth watching… When we look back on our life, in our last breaths, we will all wonder:

−Did my life mean anything?
−Was I happy?
−Was I loved?
−Did I have an impact on anyone else's life?
−Did I matter?

Before you reach that last breath ,today might be the time to make a change… **Make happiness your goal of life!**

# Quotes

[1] Hoffman, Edward. The Right to be Human: A Biography of Abraham Maslow. New York: St. Martin's Press, 1988.

[2] Maslow, A. Motivation and Personality. New York, NY: Joanna Cotler Books; 2nd edition, October 8, 1970.

[3] Maslow, Motivation… 1970.

[4] Maslow, Motivation… 1970.

[5] McLeod, S.A. "Maslow's Hierarchy of Needs." SimplyPsychology.org. Updated May 21, 2018. https://simplypsychology.org/maslow.html.

[6] Maslow, A.H. Motivation and Personality (3rd ed.). Delhi, India: Pearson Education, 1987. p 71.

[7] Nordkvist, Dieudonne D'amour, 2018.

[8] Koshuta, John. "What is Physical Health? Definition, Components & Examples." Study.com, accessed June 01, 2018. https://study.com/academy /lesson/what-is-physical-health-definition-components-examples.html.

[9] World Health Organization. Promoting Mental Health: Concepts, Emerging Evidence, Practice: Summary Report. Geneva, Switzerland: WHO and Australia Department of Mental Health and Substance Abuse, in collaboration with the Victorian Health Promotion Foundation and The University of Melbourne, 2004. NLM classification: WM 31.5. p. 10. http://www.who.int/mental_health/evidence/en/promoting_mhh.pdf.

[10] Viereck, G.S. Glimpses of the Great. New York: Macauley, 1930. p. 372–373.

[11] Wei, Marlynn MD, JD, Contributing Editor. Now and Zen: How mindfulness can change your brain and improve your health. Boston: Harvard Health Publications, 2016.

[12] Kitamura, Makiko. "Harvard Yoga Scientists Find Proof of Meditation Benefit." Bloomberg.com, November 21, 2013 (subscription required to access). https://www.bloomberg.com/news/articles/2013-11-22/harvard-yoga-scientists-find-proof-of-meditation-benefit.

[13] Wei, Now and Zen, 2016.

[14] Munroe, Myles. Understanding Your Potential: Discovering The Hidden You. Shippensburg, PA: Destiny Image Publishers; REV ed. edition, May 1, 1992.

[15] Olsen, Kaedrich. Runes for Transformation: Using Ancient Symbols to Change Your Life. Newburyport, MA: Weiser Books, August 1, 2008.

[16] The symbol + means add together. The symbol / means divided by. The symbol x means multiplied by.

[17] Sasson, Remez. "Positive Thinking Quotes." SuccessConsciousness.com, accessed May 31, 2018. https://www.successconsciousness.com/index_000033.htm.

[18] Booth, Eric. The Everyday Work of Art: Awakening the Extraordinary in Your Daily Life. iUniverse, August 9, 2001.

[19] Charles Proteus Steinmetz. Morgan, John J.B. and T. Webb Ewing. Making the Most of Your Life. Whitefish, MT: Kessinger Publishing, LLC, June 23, 2005. p. 75.

# Your assistance is appreciated

Thank you for reading this book. I hope it will help you to understand yourself better. Since we are all here in this world for a purpose, I would like to invite you to share this book with someone else. Don't keep it to yourself or put it on a shelf; lend it to a friend or give a copy away as a gift. There is someone out there who needs to read it. Help them grow, too. This new 180-Degree Rule of Sustainable Happiness model is still under construction. Please email me if you have an idea or a comment. I would greatly appreciate any feedback or understandings you wish to share: Damourus@dieudamour.com. A part of the revenue from this book will go to support IGITEGO, a non-profit organization that works for sustainable integration and inclusion in Swedish society by helping immigrants create a plan for a better life in their new homeland. www.igitego.se

# Acknowledgments

This is book is a result of many nights and days that I spent with many people. They have encouraged me to write this book, and some have taken a big part in shaping it the way it is today. Writing a book and publishing it is not easy job. But to be in a place that allows the indulgence of the time, space, and stillness needed to bring something like this to life... That, my friends and family, is a straight-up gift. This book has been crafted not just by my own hands as a single writer, but by a family of many people who want to bring sustainable happiness to the world.

*"If you want to go fast, travel alone. If you want to go far, travel together."* —African proverb

I am grateful to have been guided by kindness and love from my brainstorming friends, Nazarius Neng Bama, Simon Broomé, and my editor and linguistic assistant, Susan Uttendorfsky, along with the contribution of House of Editors. Thanks to Stamatis Iatridis for creating the cover and being the motor of this book. Without your encouragement, it wouldn't be here. Thanks to Tom Karlsson for the inlay and illustrations. To my IGITEGO TEAM family: What an incredible journey it's been. Eternal gratitude goes to you for what you are doing for our community, and for trusting me to be your leader. To my daughter in life and co-creator of ideas and business, Alexandra: I can never describe in words the gift you've been to my every breath, every moment, and every flutter of my heart. And to my best friend and godmother, Ingegärd Nyström: You inspire me to no end. Thank you for bearing up under endless nights of reading my manuscript, and for the bottomless well of hugs and kisses. To my friends, colleagues, and co-conspirators in the adventure of life, you are my heroes and you all deserve a place in this book. To you, the reader, who holds this book in your hands, thank you. I am grateful for your willingness to set aside your precious time to read it, and for your openness to exploring and sharing these words and ideas.

# About the author

D'amour Dieudonne Nordkvist Hakizimana is a Swedish national who was born in Rwanda. While pursuing his own happiness, he has traveled through many countries around the world as a teacher, speaker, coach, and social entrepreneur. He is also a founder and the CEO of IGITEGO Organization, which works for sustainable integration and inclusion in Swedish workplaces.